ARTHUR RIMBAUD
POEMS OF THE DAMNED

TRANSLATED BY JACQUES LECLERCQ
ILLUSTRATED BY STANLEY WYATT

THE PETER PAUPER PRESS
MOUNT VERNON · NEW YORK

THIS TRANSLATION
IS DEDICATED TO
MARJORIE
IN AFFECTIONATE
AND GRATEFUL
REMEMBRANCE

ARTHUR RIMBAUD *was born in* 1854: *he was an unhappy, difficult child. As a youth he ran away from home three times before he was seventeen. On these extended jaunts he was a vagrant; he almost starved, and once was jailed. But in the same years he wrote poetry, and when he was seventeen sent his now famous poem,* Drunken Ship, *to the great Verlaine. Verlaine recognized his strange genius and invited Rimbaud to join him in Paris. The two lived, traveled and fought together for more than a year; then Verlaine shot and nearly killed his friend.*

At nineteen Rimbaud gave up poetry for good, and soon afterward he disappeared. He seems to have been successively a Dutch soldier in the East Indies, a manual laborer in Europe, a wanderer in Asia Minor, and a trader in Abyssinia. Living there like a native, and trading in coffee, gold, and ivory, he became rich and influential. He re-appeared in Marseilles for an operation, an amputation, and death, in 1891.

In 1886, thinking Rimbaud dead, Verlaine had published his poems. They made a sensation in certain circles, and have never ceased to excite wonder and dismay. For Rimbaud had overlaid the sentimental, decadent imagination of a "sick" teen-ager with a violently original imagery. He became a major god of the symbolist movement.

The Illuminations *printed here will explain why the boy poet seems an ancestor of today's "beat" writer: both commit the same compulsive, irresponsible, word-outpourings. But* Rimbaud *was born with genius!*

DRUNKEN SHIP

As I descended streams impassable and dark,
I felt my haulers vanished as so many ghosts.
Redskins, shrieking, had used them for an arrow mark,
Nailing them, naked first, to many-colored posts.

Careless was I of any crew beneath the sun,
I, filled with British cottons or with Flemish grain,
When with my haulers all this blaring din was done,
The streams let me pursue my chosen ways again.

The other winter, buffeted by chopping tides,
I, duller than the minds of children, ran askew,
Madly; and no unmoored Peninsula that rides
Has known the triumphs of a like hullaballoo.

The storm hallowed my seaborne wakening by day,
Lighter than cork I danced on waves in the salt air —
Waves, those eternal victim-tossers, so to say —
Ten nights regretless of the beacon's vacuous stare.

Sweeter than flesh of sour apples to brats, the brine
Of greenish waters pierced into my pinewood shell,
Washed me of vomitings and stains of rotgut wine,
Scattering my rudder and my anchor in their swell.

Since, I have bathed in the deep Poem of the Sea,
Star-steeped, mystic, milky, whose avid waves devour
Green azures where — pallid flotsam! — rapturously
Drowned pensive men passed by me in an idle hour.

Where sudden — dyeing all the blue — delirious fires
And stately rhythms that the gleams of day invent,
Stronger than alcohol and vaster than our lyres,
The bitter fuchsia-red splotches of love ferment.

I know skies splitting into lightning day and night,
Surfs, currents, waterspouts; I know what evenings
    mean,
And dawns exalted like a people of doves, snow-white,
And I have seen at times what men think they have seen.

I have seen mystic horrors stain a setting sun,
Lighting long violet cloud-clots with a glint that flutters,
And, like mimes in most ancient dramas, the waves run
Afar, closing and opening like the slats of shutters.

I have dreamed virent nights with dazzling creamy
    snows,
Kisses that rose to the sea's eyes, slow, amorous . . .
Currents gyrating like weird saps that no man knows,
Blue-yellow wakenings of singing phosphorous.

Months long I watched reefs under the sea's
    blasting beat,
Waves pounding fierce as cow-byres in hysteric rout,
Unmindful that three Marys on translucent feet
Might curb the panting sea and gag its fiery snout.

I struck, ay, Floridas unheard of where the flowers
    blent
With panther eyes in human skins; at equinox
Rainbows as taut as bridles I saw, that never bent
Under the sea-rim as they drove their glaucous flocks.

Marshes I saw, enormous weirs whose rushes mull
A whole rotting Leviathan; I saw the spasms
Of waters crumbling into ruin amid a lull
And distances that cataracted into chasms.

Glaciers, pearl waves and silver suns, skies of live coal,
Grim wrecks, the bottom of brown gulfs their
      tenements,
Where giant snakes, which famished bugs devour
      whole,
Drop from distorted trees, shedding black olid scents.

I should have liked to show children those dolphins,
      bright
Spawn of the blue, those golden fish, those fish that
      sing . . .
Frail foamflowers blessed my aimless drifting day
      and night,
And wondrous winds at times lent me a sturdy wing.

At times — a martyr I, weary of zones and poles —
The sea, whose sobbing set my restive rolls at ease,
Raised shadowy dark flowers with yellow dry-cup bolls,
And as a woman does, I fell upon my knees. . . .

I, a peninsula, my shores kept whirligigging
The strife and dung of brawling blond-eyed birds;
      the deep
Favored my floating on, when, through my tattered
      rigging,
Drowned men swung, twirling backward, toward
      their sleep.

7

Now I, a ship lost in the hairs of coves and hurled
By hurricanes into a birdless void, sea-drunk,
What Monitor or Hansa craft in all the world
Would dream of salvaging my carcass, better sunk?

Free, smoking, rigged and tackled with a violet mist,
I, who transpierced the reddening heavens like a wall
That bears sweet condiment no poet can resist:
Lichens of sun and azure mucus flux as well;

Who, spotted with electric crescents, ran and flashed
Like a mad plank, sea horses flanking my gunwales,
When with great cudgel blows Julys pounded and
        smashed
The ultramarine skies with their tall blazing funnels;

Trembling at moans fifty leagues off borne on the
        breeze
— Rutting Behemoths or Maelstroms with furious
        threats —
Eternal weaver of blue immobilities,
I long for Europe with its ancient parapets!

I have seen isles, sidereal archipelagos
Under delirious skies for wanderers to see —
Do these depthless nights house your exile and repose,
O million golden birds, O future energy? —

But no! I have wept too much. Dawns only break
        the heart.
All moons are merciless, all suns shine ruthlessly,
Acrid love swells me with its torpid drunken smart.
O let my keel explode! let me founder at sea!

Of Europe's waters I wish but the cold black puddle
Where, under a crepuscular and fragrant sky,
A child, teeming with sadness, squats ahuddle
To launch a paper boat frail as a butterfly.

O waves, bathed in your lull, I can no longer glide
Across the wake of cargoes; I cannot eclipse
Nor cross the paths of flags and pennants in their pride,
Nor swim beneath the ghastly eyes of prison ships.

A HYPOCRITE CHASTISED

Raking, raking his amorous heart under his chaste
Black robe, . . . joyous . . . and rich kid gloves over
        his hands . . .
One day he strolled, horribly saccharine, quince-grey,
His toothless gums slobbering his faith in mucous
        strands —
One day he strolled — *Oremus!* — when a ruffian bore
Violently down on him, seizing his saintly ear,
And, voicing foul-mouthed obloquy, expertly tore
The chaste black robe from the moist flesh! O pain!
        O fear!

O punishment! His clothes were all unbuttoned as,
        aghast,
His quaking heart told the long rosary of past
Sins that had been forgiven: Saint Tartuffe turned wan,
And so confessed and raucously prayed on and on . . .
(Canonicals in hand the thief made prompt to go!)
Faugh! There Tartuffe stood stark naked from top
        to toe!

POET AGED SEVEN

Meanwhile the Mother, having closed the copy book,
Went off content and very proud, with never a look
At blue eyes under a knobbed brow—eyes of mistrust—
Her own son's soul delivered to supreme disgust.

The whole day long he sweated of obedience; very
Intelligent; and yet black *tics* and some unmerry
Traits seemed to prove he nursed acerb
     hypocrisies . . .
In gloomy corridors with faded tapestries,
Passing, he would stick out his tongue or clench
     his fists
Against his groin and see dots through his closed
     eyes' mists.
A door would open on the evening and lamplight
Showed him upstairs raging by the banister, white
 Under a gulf of roof-hung rays . . . Summers especially
Conquered and at a loss, he sought obstinately
The coolness of latrines where he could dream and
     ponder,
Tranquil, his nostrils twitching — and he, lost in
     wonder.

Winters when washed clean of the scents of afternoon
The small backyard became illumed, in a half-swoon
He would lie by the wall, buried in the black earth,
Flattening his knaggy eye as visions came to birth,
Listening to swarming bugs on thin, mangy espaliers . . .
O pity! Those brats who were his friends and familiars
Were scrawny, blank of brow, their poor eyes shot
     with blood,

Would hide thin yellow fingers ebony with mud
Under rags reeking of diarrhoea and caked with snot,
They spoke with all the mildness of an idiot;
And if before such shameless pities of distress
His mother catching him took fright, the tenderness
Of the child flung itself against her shocked surprise:
All right, so what? She would have that blue glance
    — that lies!

At seven already he wrote novels about life
In the great deserts where rapt Liberty ran rife,
Forests, suns, banks, savannahs! Inspiration came
From illustrated journals where, with cheeks aflame,
He watched *senoras* and *signoras* laugh in pride.

When mad, aged eight and dressed in calico,
    brown-eyed,
The daughter of his worker neighbors scaled the wall,
Landing upon his back so he was sure to fall,
Cornered, he under her, she shaking out her tresses,
He bit her buttocks hard for underneath her dresses
She wore no drawers — the little brute! — then he
    would feel
His body bruised by the assault of fist and heel,
And take the savors of her flesh home to remember . . .

He dreaded the wan dreary Sundays of December
When from a Bible's pages edged in cabbage-green
He read the texts, his hair reeking of brilliantine.
In bed oppressive dreams haunted his every night,
God, he loved not, but men who in the fulvous light
Black and in overalls came home amid the hum
Of the town criers who after three rolls of the drum

Read edicts that make crowds laugh, joyous, or
       groan, furious.
He dreamed of amorous meadowlands where luminous
Waves, healthy scents, pubescences of golden light
Move in their own calm rustling stir and take to flight.

And since he most enjoyed things plunged in
       somber gloom,
When he returned to his bare, closely-shuttered room,
High, blue and acridly swathed in humidity,
He would reread his novel, plotted ceaselessly,
Filled with close ochrous skies, drowned forest
       solitudes,
And flowers of flesh spread wide over sidereal
       woods,
—Vertigo and collapse, failings and rout and pity!
While he could hear the echoed rumors of the city
Below him, he would lie alone on canvas strips,
Violently foreseeing sails and distant trips!

SENSATION

In the blue summer evenings I shall go
Down paths pricked by the wheat, and, dreaming,
       tread
Soft grass cooling my weary feet below . . .
Cool rising winds shall bathe my naked head.

I shall not speak one word nor think one thing,
Infinite love shall set my heart awhirl,
I shall range far, a gipsy wandering
Through nature — glad as were I with a girl!

VERTIGO

What mean these sheets of blood and embers, O my
   heart,
To us, these thousand murders, this cacophony
Of rageful cries, sobs of all hell that rends apart
All law as Aquillo still blows on the *débris*.

And all revenge? Nothing? — Never, if it is our
Will. Perish senates, kings, tycoons — one and the same
Perish! Forever down with history, justice, power!
It is our rightful due. Blood! Blood! the golden flame!

Now let all things be terrors, vengeances and wars,
My soul! Let us turn in the wound! Warp, woof and
   stuff
Of all this world's republics, vanish! Emperors,
Armies, colonists, people — we have had enough!

Who should stir up the mad whirlwind and build
   the pyres
Save we and those we think our brothers. Furious,
O my romantic friends, let us go forth; for us
How pleasing! Never shall we work, O floods of fire!

Asia, Europe, America — sink in the void!
Cities and countries seized, oh! we shall run amuck
In vengeful warfare. We shall be destroyed.
Volcanoes will explode. As for the Ocean, struck....

Friends! Heart, surely these are my brothers as of birth:
Black strangers, if we went? Go, go, the heart resolves.
O doom! I feel myself shuddering. The ancient earth —
On me, yours more than ever, the ancient earth dissolves.

It is nothing; I am here; I am still here.

CAESAR, RAGING

This pale man walks along lawns cool and flowery,
He walks along, cigar in mouth, clad in dark sober
    dress,
This pale man recollects flowers in the Tuileries.
Sometimes a glow lights up his dull eye's glaziness.
The Emperor now is drunk from a half-century
Of orgies. He had said: *"I shall with true finesse*
Snuff freedom out like a poor candle, casually!"
But Freedom lives and he is crushed with weariness.

A captive now, oh! what name quivers on his dumb
Lips, and what pitiless regret rears its wan head?
No man shall ever know: the Emperor's eyes are dead.
(Perhaps he thinks of his bespectacled Old Chum)
He watches his cigar smoldering into blue
Spirals as once in bygone evenings at Saint Cloud.

BOHEMIAN

Fists deep in rugged pockets, on I sped,
My coat also now an ideal thing,
The skies, O Muse, to bless my wayfaring,
Ah, Lord! what splendent loves bemused my head!
Holes from my only trousers gaped like eyes,
Tom Thumb Adreams, I told my rosary
Of rhymes. The Great Bear was my hostelry.
My private stars whirred softly through the skies.

So I would listen at a roadside stop
As the September evening, drop by drop,
Distilled its wine of dew; so would I start

To rhyme as darkling shadows mimed fantastics,
Twanging, as who his lyre strings, the elastics
Of my maimed shoes, one foot against my heart.

SEEKERS AFTER LICE

When the child's brow, scratched to a smarting
    angry red,
Implores the snowy swarm of vague dreams, as he
    wails,
Two tall enchanting sisters loom beside his bed
With tapering fingers tipped with silver fingernails.

They seat the child beside a casement open wide
Over dense tangled blossoms where the air is blue
And through his heavy dew-damp hair their fingers
    glide
Tenuous, lissome, terrible and charming, too.

He listens to their breath sing, timorous and brittle,
Mellifluous, pink, earthy, and he hears the hisses
That interrupt it now and then: recovered spittle
From the red rim of lips or a desire for kisses.

Under the fragrant silences he hears their black
Lashes beat; their electric fingers in a trice
Gently amid his ashen indolences crack
As their majestic nails bring death to the small lice.

Within him now rises the wine of idleness . . .
Harmonicas, perhaps deliriously, sigh
And through his frame ruled by the sloth of the caress
The child feels a desire of weeping surge and die.

MEMORY

Clear water like the salty tears of children's weeping,
Sunlit assaults upon whiteness of women's flesh,
The silk of oriflammes with lilies in pure mesh
Under the walls some maid held in defensive keeping.

Frolic of angels; no! . . . gold, flowing on the march,
Moves its arms — heavy, black and wholly grass-
       cool. She,
Dark — the blue sky her bed's cope — calls insistently
To be curtained in the safe shade of hill and arch.

     ■ ■ ■

Eh, look! the humid pane spreads out in bubbling
       pearls!
Waters' pale depthless gold decks out each waiting bed.
The willows — whence unbridled dancing birds have
       sped —
Are the green faded pinafores of little girls.

Yellower than a louis, an eyelid warm and sweet,
See the marsh marigold — your wedding pledge,
       O bride —
From its dull mirror at high noon, envy the pride
Of the cherished rose Sphere in a sky grey with heat.

     ■ ■ ■

Madame stands too erect in the meadow nearby
Where plow the sons of toil; her parasol in hand

She tramples umbels which she finds too proud and
      bland . . .
Deep in the verdant flowering grass her children lie

Reading their red morocco book. Alas, He, light
As myriad white angels parting on the lane
Has vanished far over the mountain. She in vain,
All chilled and stiff and black, runs! after the man's
      flight.

    ■   ■   ■

Regret for arms strong and young with pure grass!
      or gold
Of April moons deep in the holy bed! How gay
The river building-yards, deserted now, a prey
To August dusks that generated all this mold.

Let her weep by the ramparts! High above its ledges
The breath of poplar trees is for the breeze alone,
Then the sheet without spring or mirror, grey as stone,
Yonder in his immobile barge an old man dredges.

    ■   ■   ■

Toy of this mournful water eye, ever I fail
(O rooted boat! O arms too short!) to pluck the two
Blossoms: the yellow one, a nuisance, or the blue,
Amicable to waters glazed and ashen-pale.

Ah, dust of willow trees that wings shake as they climb,
Roses of reeds long since abandoned to devouring,
My boat is still stuck fast, its useless cable scouring
Deep down this rimless water eye — amid what slime!

HAPPINESS

O seasons, O *châteaux*,
All souls bear their flaws, I know.

That magic study I pursued
Of Happiness no men elude!

O hail to him each time we hear
The crowing Gallic chanticleer.

But I shall nurse desires no more
Now he is my life's governor.

That spell! It seized body and soul,
My efforts scattered by its toll.

Who feels what my words signify?
It causes them to flee and fly.

(The hour alas! of flight's last breath
Shall also be the hour of death!)

O seasons, O *châteaux*.

THE DISMAYED

Black in the snow and in the mist
By the grilled window now aglow,
    Their scuts forming a ring,

Kneeling, five brats — O misery! —
See the blond heavy bread and see
    The Baker laboring.

They see a strong white arm that stirs
The greyish paste which it transfers
    To a bright cavity.

They hear the good bread baking while
The Baker with a chubby smile
    Hums out an ancient glee.

They huddle up, none moves, intent
Upon the breath of the red vent
    Warm as a breast is warm.

When for some midnight feast the bread,
Shaped as a *brioche*, shows its head,
    Then its whole tempting form,

When under the beams' smoke and dust
Songs rise from every fragrant crust
    And many a cricket chatters,

As this warm hole breathes life and light
Their hearts are filled with rapt delight
    Under their rags and tatters.

They feel they live a second time,
A Christ-child, each, covered with rime,
    These five poor little souls,

Each pressing a small rosy snout
Against the bars, and, with a pout,
    Grumbling between the holes.

Fatuous, they say their prayers, and crane
Towards these lights which once again
    Unfold as heavens unfold,

So tensely that their breeches split,
And that their shirts flutter a bit
    As winter winds blow cold.

WINTER DREAM

Winters, we'll ride in a small train as pink as roses,
    With cushions of soft blue.
We'll be so comfortable! A kissing nest reposes
    In each snug nook for you.
You'll close your eyes lest you see the grimaces
    Night's shades make as they swell
In quarrelsome monstrosities with populaces
    Of wolves and fiends from hell.

You shall feel your soft cheek brushed by a tiny
    speck,
A little kiss like a mad spider on your neck —
    At its gossamer touch
You'll say: "*You might look for the horrid thing
    at least!*"
And we'll spend quite some time before we find
    this beast
        Which travels very much.

SEASCAPE

Chariots of silver and copper,
Prows of steel and silver
Beat the foam
And raise the stubs of bramble.
The currents of the wasteland
And the immense ruts of their ebb
Veer away eastward in a circle
Toward the pillars of the forest,
Toward the piles of the jetty
Whose angle is buffeted by whirlwinds of light.

THE BALL OF THE HANGED

Under the kindly one-armed gallows
They dance, they dance, the paladins,
Thin paladins the Devil hallows,
The skeletons of Saladins.

Master Beélzebub tugs deftly at the black
Neckties of his thin puppets grinning at the moon,
And with his shoe he deals them a smart backhand
    smack,
Making them dance and dance to an old Christmas tune!

And the small puppets intertwine their scrawny arms.
Like so many black organs, chests that are laid bare
And that were once hugged tight by damsels of
    rare charms
Knock long — in hideous amour — together there.

Hurrah! Blithe dancers, who have lost your
    paunches, prance!
Caper now, for the stage is wide, the fun begins!
Hop, let none know: is this a battle or a dance?
Beélzebub in fury scrapes his violins.

O stout heels, not one puppet ever wore out sandal!
Though almost all have shed their shirts of skin at that!
The not-too-awkward rest may be seen without scandal,
Upon these skulls the snow applies a hoary hat.

To these cleft pates the raven furnishes a plume,
A patch of flesh shakes on their thin chins. You
    would say,
As they go whirling round in dark *mêlées* of doom,
Stiff knights who clash in armors of *papier mâché*.

Hurrah, the north wind howls at the Skeleton Ball,
The gallows' roar is like an iron organ's swell!
From violet woods to the horizon, the wolves bawl
In antiphon. The skies are red as those of Hell.

Ho, there, shake up these dull captains in their dismay
Who with thick broken fingers pawkily unthread
A rosary of love on their wan vertebrae!
This is no monastery, O ye heedless dead!

But suddenly a tall crazed skeleton appears
From out the *danse macabre* he leaps through the
    red sky,
Borne by his own momentum as a horse that rears
He still feels at his neck the rope he was hanged by.

Clenching ten fingers on his crackling thigh, uncouth,
With grating cries that sound like a sharp snickering,
Much as a mountebank re-entering his booth,
He leaps back to the ball as all the dead bones sing.

> *Under the kindly one-armed gallows*
> *They dance, they dance, the paladins,*
> *Thin paladins the Devil hallows,*
> *The skeletons of Saladins.*

MICHEL AND CHRISTINE

Oh damn! Suppose the sun forsakes these shores
    and stops!
Flee, O bright deluge! Here are roads with cooling
    shades.
The storm at outset casts its earliest big drops
Over the ancient courtyard and the willow glades.

A hundred lambs, bright soldiers of the idyll, flee!
Flee from the aqueducts and from the scrawny heather,
Plain, desert, meadowland, horizons duteously
Are at the red ablutions of the raging weather.

Black sheepdog and dark shepherd (his coat swells
    over him)
Flee in the hour when lightning flashes on the heights,
White flock, when you behold shadows and sulphur
    swim,
Try to go down to shelter in more favored sites.

But I, O Lord, behold my spirit winging high
Towards heaven's frozen icy-red under the wan
Celestial clouds coursing across the air and fly
Over fivescore Solognes long as an *Eisenbahn*.

Behold thousands of wolves and thousands of wild
    seeds
Borne hence on this religious afternoon of storm
Which does not fail to love bearbine and other weeds
Over old Europe when a hundred hordes shall swarm.

These moonlights on unending moors! Over the land
Warriors of ruddy mien, eyeing the dark skies, ride
Slowly on their pale chargers in their knightly pride
As stones go ringing under this illustrious band.

Shall I see the gold wood, and the vale, clear and sweet,
The blue-eyed Bride; O Gaul, the red-faced man,
    my friend,
And the white Paschal Lamb at their belovèd feet
And Michel and Christine — and Christ, the idyll's end?

EVIL

While all day long the guns spit red gobs, shell on shell,
Whistling through infinite blue skies ere they expire,
While near a mocking king amid this din of hell
Scarlet or green battalions crumble under fire,
While a fierce madness grips and crushes man and
    earth,
Leaving a smoking heap where myriad men should be,
— Poor dead, in summer, in the grass . . . and in
    your worth,
Nature, who moulded all these men in sanctity:

There is a god scorns damask cloths, rich vestments
    and
Altars and incense and great chalices of gold,
And who, lulled by hosannas, slumbers, bland,
But who awakes when mothers gathered in their cold
Anguish, under their old black bonnets, weep for grief,
Tending a copper from a knotted handkerchief.

VENUS EMERGING

As from a green tin coffin, so a woman's head
Emerges slowly — her dark hair heavily oiled —
From an old bathtub. Dull and ponderous as lead,
Revealing deficits ill-patched and not unsoiled,
The fat grey neck, then the broad salient omoplates,
Then the short back at once convex and cavernous,
Her subcutaneous grease spreads out in flattened plates,
The roundness of her loins gathers an impetus.

Her spine is somewhat red. The whole gives forth a stink
Horrible, strangely. All the freaks of this live sump
Should be seen through a magnifying glass, I think.
Two words engraved upon her back read: *Clara Venus*.
The whole frame stirs and tenders its vast rump,
Beautiful hideously with ulcers of the anus.

SHAME

So long as no blade shall have cut
Away that bundle called the brain,
Green white and fatty, boasting but
The selfsame vapors ever again

(Ah, really he should amputate
His nose, his lips, his ears for us,
His belly, too! and abdicate
His two long legs! O marvelous!)

But no, this should be modified:
The blade has left his head uncut,
The stones have not smashed in his side,
The flame has not consumed his gut,

Wherefore, I think, given such neglect,
This nuisance-child, this oaf, should be
Studious to practice and respect
Ruse, fraudulence and treachery,

And like a Rocky Mountain cat
To make all spheres stink to the skies . . .
Yet at his deathbed, Lord, grant that
Somewhere a humble prayer arise.

A COMEDY OF KISSES

She was excessively undressed
And the great trees, eschewing fear
Of indiscretion, slily pressed
Their foliage near and very near.

Her hands linked, she lolled back at leisure
Half-naked in my easy chair,
Quavering on the floor for pleasure
Her slight feet flashed, fair and more fair.

I looked at a small ray meanwhile,
A leafy waxen ray; and I
Marked how it fluttered in her smile
And on her breast — a rosebush fly!

I kissed her slender ankles till
Her undue giggling, clear and deft,
Tripped saucily in trill on trill
As crystal laughter from a cleft.

Her dainty toes sought to retreat
Under her shirt. "*Stop!*" Her assent
To my first rashness being complete,
Her laughter was my punishment.

Under my lips, her poor eyes throbbed,
I kissed them quietly at will
As back and forth her light head bobbed:
"*Oh, that is sweet, and sweeter still!*

"*Monsieur, look here . . .*" Then, all delight,
I flung my kisses on her breast,
The volley made her laugh outright
In healthy peals that acquiesced. . . .

She was excessively undressed
And the great trees, eschewing fear
Of indiscretion, slily pressed
Their foliage near and very near.

CROWS

Lord, in the vast plain's coldest hours,
When in the stricken thorps the long
Angeluses have ceased their song,
Over a nature stripped of flowers,
From out Thy skies in flight on flight,
Let loved delicious crows alight.

Strange hosts cawing grim threnodies,
The cold wind storms your every nest,
Down yellowed streams, you, without rest,
Along roads with old calvaries,
Over the ditches, pools and holes,
Scatter, then rally back in shoals.

Throng in your thousands these December
French fields where lie the lately slain,
Turn, turn and then return again
That every passer-by remember:
Cry out his duty with harsh breath,
Lugubrious sable bird of death!

But, saints of heaven! atop the oak,
A mast lost in the dwindling day,
Spare ye the sweet blackcap of May
For those deep in the wood whose yoke
Inflicts on them the hopeless sorrow
Of a defeat without a morrow.

ROMANCE

No lad at seventeen is earnest in his ways.
On some fine evening, pooh! for beer or lemonade,
For dazzling candelabra in loud cafés! —
You stroll under green lindens on the promenade.

How fragrant on sweet nights of June the lindens are!
Sometimes you close your eyes in the soft air, you hear
The wind, burdened with noise — the city is not far —
You smell the scent of vineyards and the scent of beer.

      ■ ■ ■

Now you perceive a tiny square of dark blue felt
Framed by a little branch, and in the evening light
The wayward star stitched onto it begins to melt
With gentle tremors; small it is and very white.

June nights! You let them make you tipsy. Seventeen!
The sap is pure champagne; as heady as its froth.
Your mind goes rambling off; you feel a kiss between
Your lips, palpitant there, like a small summer moth.

      ■ ■ ■

Your crazy heart goes Crusoeing through fond romances
When, in the wan light of the street lamp where you
     strayed,
A girl walks with a grace that piques and that entrances
Under her father's collar and its frightening shade.

Of course she finds you utterly unknowing while
Her light shoes patter on. How winsomely she trips!

She turns, alert, with a quick move and a half-smile,
And then the *cavatinas* die upon your lips.

■   ■   ■

You are in love, rented until September 1,
You are in love; your sonnets make her laugh; polite
But firm, your friends abandon you; you are no fun . . .
—And then — one evening — the adored one deigns
        to write.

That evening you return to the dazzling cafés,
You order pints of peer or quarts of lemonade —
No lad of seventeen is earnest in his ways
When the green lindens rustle on the promenade.

THE FAUN

Behind a screen of greengold mottled foliage, deep
In an uncertain thicket, dense and blossoming
With twinkling flowers where the kiss lies sound
        asleep —
Alert and piercing the exquisite broidery,

A startled faun shows his slant eyes weirdly ashine,
Then bites the crimson flowers with his white teeth;
        and after,
Sanguinolous and brownish like an ancient wine,
His lips under the boughs burst into strident laughter.

When, deft and fleet as any squirrel he has fled,
His laughter trembles still on each leaf, and you see
The woods' gold kiss, which had been dreaming
        peacefully,
Terrified by a chaffinch winging overhead.

LACRIMA

Far from the birds, the cattle, the village girls I was,
I drank as I crouched down amid the flowering heather,
Surrounded by light groves of softspun hazel trees
In the green afternoon's lukewarm and hazy weather.

What was it I could drink from this same River Oise:
—Elms without voice, bottomless turf and skies beset—
What draft was it I drew out of my kalo gourd?
Some flavorless gold liquor that induces sweat . . .

As such, what a poor signboard for an inn were I!
Then the storm raged till night. Then what continuations
Of somber lands, of lakes, of rods and poles passed by,
Of colonnades in the blue night, of railway stations.

The waters of the groves were lost in virgin sand,
Heaven's wind cast icicles on marshes black as ink.
Gold! like a fisher of gold or shells upon the strand,
Imagine! There I was, and had no wish to drink!

SLEEPER IN THE VALLEY

A gap of green through which the singing waters glide,
Madly entangling rags of silver with the grass,
Where sunlight sparkles, mirrored by the mountainside,
A little vale where light bubbles like freshblown glass:
Bareheaded, mouth agape, a youthful soldier lies,
His neck dipped in the cool blue cress, and here,
     for hours

Slumbers, sprawled out upon the turf under the skies,
Pale is his greensward bed where light rains down
 in showers.

He sleeps, feet deep in the gladioli, a child
Fever-spent on a sickbed ... Nature, O be mild,
Rock this cold body in the warmest of your cribs ...
Scents, rising, fail to thrill his nostrils as, at rest,
He slumbers in the sun, one hand upon his breast ...
On his right side two holes gape red between his ribs.

VOWELS

Vowels: A black, E white, I red, U green, O blue:
Some day I shall reveal your latent complement ...
A, black and hairy corset of bright flies intent
On bumbling over excremental residue,
Abyss of darkness; E, pureness of steam and tent,
Proud glacier spears, white kings' umbels cooled by
 the dew,
I, crimson, blood hawked up, sweet lips smiling anew
In wrath or in the rapture of a penitent.

U, cycles, virid seas in their divine vibration,
Peace of green pastures sown with beasts, of
 meditation,
Alchemy's wrinkles stamped on brows studious and
 wise,
O, clarion supreme, strange stridors it disperses,
Silences crossed by Angels and by Universes,
The Omega — the ray of violet in One's Eyes.

OPHELIA

On calm black tides where stars slumber and
    moonlight pales,
Like a vast lily in blossom, white Ophelia floats,
Floats very slowly, slowly, in her virgin veils.
Far off the woodland horns echo the mort's last notes.

For ten times fivescore years Ophelia in her sadness
Passes, a white wraith, down the long black stream;
    and these
Ten long times fivescore years have heard her gentle
    madness
Humming its wistful ballad to the evening breeze.

The wind kisses her breasts, and, as corollas spread,
So her great veils which the cool water lulls and kneads;
The shuddering willow trees weep over her wan head,
Her wide pale brow dreaming sweeps by the bowing
    reeds.

Bruised lilies sigh around her as slowly she swings
Sidewise. At times she wakes sleeping alders that hold
Some nest . . . there is a fluttering of little wings . . .
And a mysterious song rains down from stars of gold!

    ■ ■ ■

O pale Ophelia, fair as snow is fair, you died
A child, the flotsam of streams flowing steadily,
Because the winds from the Norwegian mountainside
Whispered to you the bitterness of being free,

Because an unknown breath, twisting your trailing hair,
Fulfilled your dreamy mind with new strange
    thoughts and sights,
Because your heart heard Nature's voice in the dim
    prayer
Of wailing trees and in the sighing of still nights.

Because the voice of seas, choking in death's last fear,
Shattered your child heart, all too human and too sweet,
Because one April morn a pale tall cavalier,
A sorry madman, sat in silence at your feet.

Heaven, Love, Freedom? — mad girl! what a dream
    to seek!
You melted to him as snows melt when hot flames rise,
Your lofty visions strangled you ere you could speak,
Fearsome Infinity bewildered your blue eyes.

    ■ ■ ■

The Poet says that when stars shine and the moon sails,
Nightly you come to cull the flowers you once called
    stilly,
And that he saw the waters bear the heavy veils
Of white Ophelia floating like a giant lily.

QUATRAIN

The star wept rosy through the bosom of your ears,
White rolls the infinite over your nape and back,
The sea pearled brown on your red nipples through
    the years,
On your sovereign flanks the Son of man bleeds black.

SITTERS IN THE LIBRARY

Black moles on pitted skins . . . their eyes circled
    with green
Rings . . . weazened fingers clutching at femoral bones . . .
Sinciputs caked with vague crustinesses, obscene
As leprous weed-blossoms over an old wall's stones.

In epileptic loves, each has grafted apace
His eerie carcass to the great black skeleton
Of a tall chair round whose rachitic bar they brace
Their feet morning and noon and evening, on and on.

Each oldster always braided to his chair well knows
The feel of summer suns glossing a hide that glowed,
Or he has eyed the panes where fade December snows
Trembling with the heart-rending tremors of the toad.

And their seats are indulgent to them: browned and
    coddled,
The straw yields gladly to the angles of their reins,
The soul of ancient suns lights up again, tight-swaddled
In these tressed heads of wheat where once fermented
    grains.

The sitters, knees drawn up to teeth, green pianists,
    drum
With tenuous fingers on the bottoms of their chairs,
Their noodles drool to rhythmic swells of love that
    come
As they hear plashing barcarolles and dolesome airs.

Noon. Lunch break. Don't make them get up!
    Catastrophe!

They surge with mews and pules like alley-cats one
    smacks,
Slowly squaring their shoulders (o asperity!)
Trousers ballooning freely over swelling backs.

And you can hear them clumping, clumping their
    splay feet
And knocking their bald pates against the somber walls,
The buttons of their clothes are fulvous eyes that meet
And hook your glance out of long corridors and halls.

And their killing invisible hands! . . . After which,
Back from their lunch they gaze with poisoned eyes
    of haters
Such as spark suffering glances from a beaten bitch . . .
Watching, you sweat as one caught in atrocious craters.

Seated again, each fist drowned in a dirty cuff,
They think of those who made them come here for
    their sins,
From morn to night clusters of tonsils swell and puff
To bursting point under their puny stunted chins.

When austere sleep lowers their visors, lo! they dream,
Heads on their arms, each of his fecundated seat,
Sweet darling little chairs lined up in rows that gleam
In front of desks and tables equally as sweet.

Flowers of ink spit pollens, comma shaped, that rise
Along the squatting chalices of inkpots, safe
As are gladioli by moveless dragonflies —
Against the prickles of the straw, their members
    chafe. . . .

MOVEMENT

The oscillation of the riverfalls on the bank,
The abyss at the stern post,
The celerity of the slope,
The enormous leap-frogging of the current,
By means of incredible lights
And chemical novelties
Lead the travelers who are surrounded by
        whirlwinds of the valley
And waterspouts of the *strom*.

These are the conquerors of the world
Seeking personal chemical fortune;
Sport and comfort travel in their company;
They bring with them onto this ship
The education of races, of classes and of beasts:
Repose and vertigo
With diluvian light,
With terrible evenings of study.

For, from the chatter amid apparatuses, blood,
        flowers, fire, jewels,
From the accounts bandied on this fleeing ship,
You see — rolling like a dike beyond the hydraulic
        propelling road,
Monstrous, lighting up endlessly — you see their
        stock of studies;
They, hidden in the harmonic ecstasy
And the heroism of discovery.

From the most startling of atmospheric accidents
A youthful couple finds isolation on the pump box

(Is it ancient savagery that we forgive?)
To sing and take their stand.

YOUNG COUPLE

The room lies open to a sea-blue turquoise sky.
No space at all — chests, coffers, hutches everywhere.
The wall outside is full of snakevine, thick and high,
Whence red gums of hobgoblins quiver in the air.

Surely the pawky strategy of Djinns abides
In this futile expense and litter. (Truth to tell,
It is the kindly Afric fairy that provides
The mulberries — and cobwebs in each nook as well!)

Enter some characters — sulky godmothers these —
On the buffets in shafts of light from the warm sun,
And here they stay. The harum-scarum couple flees
Giddily off — leaving what should be done undone!

The thieving wind blows at all times to fleece the groom
Whenever he is absent from his lodgings here,
Even the water sprites sow havoc and spread doom,
Roaming around the alcove's purlieus without fear.

At night their woman friend, ho! ho! The honeymoon
Will cull their smiles and fill the sky with countless flat
Bandeaux of shining copper, and too soon, too soon,
It shall be theirs to cope with the insidious rat!

If no pale Jack-o'-Lantern comes to harry them
Like a loud gunshot after evensong is said —
O all ye white and holy Ghosts of Bethlehem,
Enchant their window in its glowing blue instead!

ETERNITY

It is recovered, see!
What? — Eternity.
It is the sea
Fused with the sun!

Soul, O sentinel,
Let us murmur the vow
Of night so null
And day so flaming now.

With human opinions,
With common energy,
You break; your pinions
Soar accordingly.

Since from yourselves alone,
O embers of satin, fast
Duty breathes out and none
Can say: at last!

No hope there, and thence
No orietur pure,
Knowledge, skill, patience,
Torment is all too sure.

It is recovered, see!
What? — Eternity.
It is the sea
Fused with the sun.

ILLUMINATIONS

AFTER THE FLOOD

So soon as the idea of the Flood had settled:

A hare stopped dead in the sainfoin patch amid the swaying bellflowers and he said his prayer (as he stared through the spider's web) to the rainbow.

Oh, the precious stones that lurked in hiding, and oh! the flowers that were already beginning to gaze wide-eyed about them.

In dirty Main Street, stalls were being set up. Boats were being hauled to the sea; and the sea was high-tiered as on the background of ancient chromos.

Blood flowed at Bluebeard's, and in the slaughter houses, and in circuses where the seal of God Almighty made even the windows turn pale. Blood and milk flowed aplenty.

Beavers began building big dams. In little bars and grills, coffee fumed out of goblets in metal canisters.

In the great glass house with its panes still dripping, children in mourning dress looked at marvelous pictures.

A door banged shut. In the village square, the little boy twirled his arms around and around, under the dazzling shower of rain, in a gesture understood of all weather vanes and all chanticleers on belfries everywhere in the world.

Madame X—— installed a piano in the High Alps. Masses and First Communions were celebrated before the hundred thousand altars of the cathedral.

Caravans set out abroad. And the Splendide-Hôtel was erected out of a chaos of ice and polar night.

Ever since, the Moon heard jackals yowling across deserts of thyme and eclogues in clogs creaking in the orchard. Then, in the budding violet grove, Eucharis told me that it was spring.

O pond, gush forth; Foam, roll over the bridge and high atop the woodland; O sable palls and organs, O lightning and thunder, arise and bowl forward; O waters and sorrows arise and create new Floods.

For since the Floods have abated — oh, the precious stones going underground and oh, the blossoming flowers! — everything is mortally boring! And the Queen, the Sorceress who kindles her fire in an earthen pot, will never tell us what she knows and what we do not know.

CHILDHOOD

That idol with black eyes and yellow mane,
without parents or court, nobler than any
fable whether Mexican or Flemish! His do-
main insolent in its azure and verdure runs
over sea beaches baptised by shipless waves
with names that are fiercely Greek, Slavic or
Celtic.

At the edge of the forest — dreamflowers
tinkle, burgeon and burst into light — the
maiden with orange lips, her knees crossed in
the luminous flood that wells up from the
fields, offers her nakedness which is shaded,
threaded and costumed by rainbows and flora
and the seas.

There are ladies strolling on terraces close to
the seashore, baby girls and titan women,
superbly black in the foamy verdigris moss,
jewels erect on the rich earth of groves and of
small thawed-out gardens; there are young
mothers and big sisters whose eyes are full of
pilgrimages, sultanas, princesses tyrannical in
their gait and their costume, little foreign girls
and persons that are mildly unhappy.

Oh, how boring the hour of the "dear body"
and the "dear heart!"

■　■　■

She it is, the little girl lying dead behind the
rose bushes. —The youthful Mama, likewise

deceased, walks down the flight of steps. — The cousin's barouche creaks on the sand. — The little brother (he is in the Indies!) is there in a meadow studded with carnations facing the setting sun. — The old people too, who were buried standing erect in the rampart covered with gillyflowers. . . .

Swarms of golden leaves surround the General's house. They are in the southland. — You follow the red road to reach the empty inn. The *château* is for sale, the shutters have been taken down. — The priest must have made off with the key to the church.

Around the park, the keepers' lodges are uninhabited. The fences are so high that you can see only the rustling tree tops. Besides, there is nothing to be seen behind those fences anyhow.

The meadows range up towards hamlets that have no roosters or anvils. The sluice gate is open. O the Calvaries and the windmills of the desert, the islands and the hayricks!

■ ■ ■

In the wood there is a bird whose song stops you in your tracks and makes you blush. There is a clock that never strikes. There is a hollow with a nest of white beasts. There is a cathedral which slopes down and a lake that soars upward. There is a little carriage abandoned in the coppice or rolling beribboned down the path. There is a troupe of small actors in costume; they can be glimpsed on the road from the edge of the wood.

And, finally, when you are hungry and thirsty, there is some one there to chase you away.

■ ■ ■

I am the saint at his prayers on the terrace like those peaceful beasts that pasture all the way to the sea of Palestine. I am the savant in the dark armchair. Branches and rain beat against the casement window of my library. I am the pedestrian on the highway that skirts the dwarf woodland. The roar of the sluices covers the sound of my footsteps. For long and long I see the melancholy laundering of the setting sun. I might well be the child forsaken on a jetty which is floating out to the high seas or the little farm hand following the lane whose brow touches the very skies.

The paths are rugged, the hillocks covered with broom. The air is motionless. How far away the birds are, how distant the springs!

As I move forward, it can only be towards the world which is coming to an end.

■ ■ ■

At long last, let them rent me this whitewashed tomb with its cement lines in relief very far underground.

I rest my elbows on the table, the lamp shines

very brightly on these newspapers I am idiotic enough to re-read and on these wholly uninteresting books.

At an enormous distance above my subterranean sitting room, houses take root and fogs gather. The mud is red or black. O monstrous city, O night without end!

Somewhat less high, there are sewers. At the sides there is nothing save the thickness of the globe. Perhaps it is at these levels that moons and comets meet and seas and fables come together.

During my hours of bitterness, I imagine balls of sapphire and of metal. I am lord of the silence about me. Why should the semblance of an air shaft turn pale under one corner of the vault?

RUTS

On the right, summer dawn awakens the leaves and the mists and the rumors that rise from this corner of the park; on the left, the slopes enfold the myriad swift runnels of the wet road in an embrace of violet shadows.

Behold a parade of faeryland delights! Ay, here we watch floats stream by bearing animals of gilded wood; here are poles and canvas hangings bespattered with variegated colors, whirling by to the double gallop of fivescore piebald circus horses; and here are children and men riding by, mounted on the most astounding of beasts.

And twenty embossed vehicles, decked with flowers and flags, like the coaches of yore or like curricles out of fairy tales, filled with children dressed up for a suburban pastorale.

And here are coffins, even, under their night-black canopies, raising their ebony plumes as they roll along to the trot of huge sable and cobalt mares. . . .

MYSTIQUE

On the slope of the hill angels twirl their woolen robes in grasslands of steel and of emerald. Meadows of flames leap up to the crown of the hillock. On the left the leaf-mold of the ridge is trampled underfoot by all the murderers and battles that ever were, and here all disastrous tumults describe their appointed curves.

And while the band atop the picture is formed by the eddying and whirling of seashells and of human nights —

The flowery softness of the stars and of the night and of all the rest descends opposite the slope and settles there like a basket against our face and makes of the abyss below a bed of blue and perfumed blossoms.

MORNING OF DRUNKEN RAPTURE

O *my* Good, and O *my* Beautiful, and O heart-rending fanfare over which I do not stumble! O faery hobby horse and O rack of sorcery! Hurrah for the incredible work being accomplished and for the marvelous body accomplishing it, and this for the first time!

The thing began amid the laughter of children and even so shall it end. This poison shall endure in all our veins even when, the fanfare circling, we shall be re-committed to the age-old cacophony. But O now — we so worthy of such torments — let us even now fervently gather up that superhuman promise which was made to our body and our soul in their creation. That promise which is madness unalloyed.

Elegance, knowledge, violence? It was promised us that the tree of good and evil would be buried in darkness, and that tyrannical conventions would be deported so that we might arise, bearing our very pure gift of love.

This began with instances of disgust and it ended — we unable immediately to pounce upon this eternity — it ended with a phantasmagoria of fragrances.

Laughter of little children, discretion of slaves, austerity of virgins, horror of the faces and objects hereabouts, be you all thrice-blessed in memory of this vigil. It began in wholesale boorishness, and look! it is ending with angels of flame and ice.

Little lightsome drunken vigil, holy be your name! And this if only because of the mask with which we have been invested thanks to you. You are method and we affirm your name; we are not forgetting that yesterday you glorified each of our ages. In the poison we trust. We know how to devote our entire lives day in, day out.

Now is the hour of the *Assassins*.

DEMOCRACY

"The banner suits this obscene landscape and our jargon drowns out the drum. In centers of civilization, we shall foster the most cynical prostitution. We shall massacre all logical revolts.

"Let us go to pepper-hot and rain-sodden lands, at the service of the most monstrous industrial or military exploitations.

"Farewell until we meet again here or no matter where. Conscripts of good will, we shall practice a ferocious philosophy; we shall be ignorant in the matter of science and wily where our comforts are concerned, and let

this world as it is die like a dog! This marks
the true trend of progress.

"Forward, march!"

LIVES

O the enormous avenues of the Holy Land, the
terraces of the Temple! What has happened to
the Brahmin who commented on the Book of
Proverbs for my benefit? I can still see even
the old women of those times and of that yonder! I recall silvery hours and sunshine over
there by the riverbanks. I recall the hand of a
girl cupping my shoulder and our caresses as
we stood on plains redolent of pepper.

A flight of scarlet pigeons thunders round and
round my thoughts. An exile here, I used to
have a stage upon which to enact the dramatic
masterpieces of all literatures. I would show
you incredible riches. I note the history of the
treasures that you discovered, and I see the
results! Men disdain my wisdom just as they
disdain chaos. What is my nothingness against
the stupor that awaits you?

■ ■ ■

An inventor, I, a discoverer far more deserv-
ing than all those who have gone before me;
I am even a musician for I have unearthed
something akin to the key to love. At present
a squire on a dour estate under a sober sky,
I try to arouse my interest by remembering my

beggarly childhood, my apprenticeship for which I arrived in wooden shoes, polemics of all sorts, five or six instances of widowhood, and various carousals when my stubborn head saved me from rising to the diapason of my fellows.

I do not regret my past share of divine glee; the sober air of this harsh landscape fosters my dreadful scepticism very actively. But since this scepticism can henceforth no longer be put to use, and since, moreover, I am sworn to a new turmoil, I await the moment when I shall turn into a very harmful madman.

■ ■ ■

In an attic where I was shut in when I was twelve years old, I learned to know the world. I illustrated the comedy of human existence. In a wine cellar I learned history. In a city of the north, during some nocturnal celebration, I met all the women of the old master-painters. In an ancient Paris arcade, I was taught the classical sciences. In a magnificent residence encompassed by the entire Orient, I accomplished my immense work and I lived out the days of my illustrious retirement.

I have brewed and stirred up my own blood. My duty has been recommitted into my own hands. But I must not think of that any more. Truly, I belong that side of the grave and I have no messages to bring to you.

VAGABONDS

O lamentable brother, what ghastly nights of sleeplessness I owed him. According to him I was not following this enterprise fervently, I had made game of his infirmity, and through my fault we were to return into exile and bondage. He presumed that I bore a jinx and an innocence, both very bizarre, and, to this argument, he added troublous reasons.

I used to answer this satanic doctor with a sneer and I ended up by moving over to the window. From there, beyond a landscape streaked with chaplets of rare music, I used to create the phantoms of our pending nocturnal superfluities.

After this vaguely hygienic pastime, I used to stretch out on my pallet and almost every night, no sooner was I asleep than the poor wretch would get up, his mouth putrid and his eyes goggling (such as he dreamed himself to be) to drag me into the room where he blared out his idiot dream of sorrow.

In point of fact I had, in all sincerity, sworn to bring him back to his primitive state, that of a scion of the Sun.

And so, fortified by the wine of caverns and the biscuit of highroads, we wandered on and on, I in a hurry to find the place and the formula.

FLOWERS

From amid silken cordons, grey gauzes and verdant velours and crystal disks that blacken as bronze in the sun, from a golden tier I watch the purple foxglove blossoming out on a carpet of silver filigree, of eyes and of hair.

I see yellow doubloons scattered over agate bases, and mahogany pillars supporting a dome of emeralds, and bouquets of white satin, and tenuous sprays of rubies surrounding the white and yellow water lilies.

Like a god with enormous blue eyes and loins of snow, sea and sky lure the crowd of youthful and powerful roses toward terraces of marble.

KNOCKABOUT SHOW

Before the show starts in the booth, we see these very sturdy rogues giving a side show. They have no needs and they are in no hurry to apply their dazzling faculties and their understanding of your consciences. What ripe, what mature men they are! Eyes glazed with hebetude much as a summer night, red and black, tri-colored, fashioned of steel pricked with golden stars. And those faces, those physiognomies that are wizened, mis-shaped, leaden, blanched and blazing! And those madcap tones in their hoarse voices! Ah, the cruel gait of tawdry theatrical finery!

Some of these fellows are young — how would they view Cherubin, that symbol of amorous youth? They are equipped with terrifying voices and with a few somewhat perilous resources. Their employers send them into town, bedizened with vomit-making luxury, to indulge and be indulged in backscuttling.

O the most violent Paradise of rabid grimaces! You cannot compare these fellows with Fakirs and other stage buffoonery. In costumes they have improvised, they perform sentimental love ballads, high tragedies of rogues and demigods more soulful than history and religion have ever been — the whole with the aftertaste of a nightmare.

Chinese, Hottentots, Gypsies, crackpots, hyenas, Molochs, outworn dementias, sinister demons, they mingle popular maternal stunts with bestial attitudes and bestial fondling. They would interrupt new plays and songs to squeeze tears from the eyes of maidens. They are master jugglers, they transmogrify place and persons, then batten upon magnetic comedy. Their eyes blaze, their blood sings, their bones swell as tears and red runnels flow down their cheeks. Their mockery or the terror they inspire can last one minute or months at a time. I alone hold the key to this raree show.